MAID OF HONOR
Planner

BELONGS TO: ....

Dates to Remember

Wedding Date: _____

Save the Dates Mailed By: _____

Dress Shopping (Bride): _____

Dress Shopping (Bridesmaids): _____

Invitations Mailed By: _____

Bridal Shower: _____

Dress Alterations: _____

Bachelorette Party: _____

_____

_____

_____

_____

_____

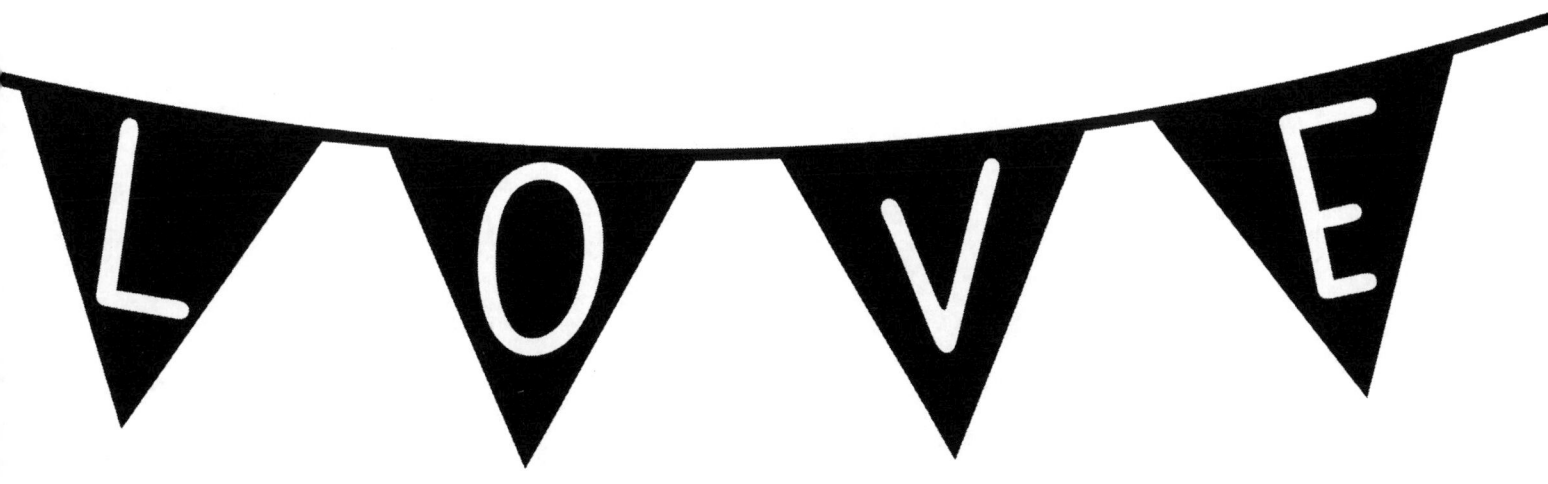

Wedding
Planning

Wedding Planning Checklist

12-18 MONTHS BEFORE THE WEDDING

- ☐ Help bride shop for wedding dress
- ☐ Help shop for bridesmaid dresses
- ☐ Help scout for vendors
- ☐
- ☐
- ☐
- ☐

NOTES

3-6 MONTHS BEFORE THE WEDDING

- ☐ Start planning bachelorette/bridal party
- ☐ Consult with bridesmaids
- ☐ Coordinate bridesmaids' hair, make-up
- ☐
- ☐
- ☐
- ☐

NOTES

2-3 MONTHS BEFORE THE WEDDING

- ☐ Shop for wedding gift
- ☐ Schedule alteration appointments
- ☐ Book hair and make up appointments
- ☐
- ☐
- ☐

NOTES

Wedding Planning Checklist

1 MONTH BEFORE THE WEDDING

- [ ] Write toast for wedding day
- [ ] Finalize your accessories/hair style/other
- [ ] Tell others about the wedding registry
- [ ] Host a bridal shower
- [ ]
- [ ]
- [ ]

NOTES

SHORTLY BEFORE THE WEDDING

- [ ] Keep bridesmaids up to date on plans
- [ ] Host a bachelorette party
- [ ]
- [ ]
- [ ]
- [ ]
- [ ]

NOTES

WEDDING DAY

- [ ] Help bride get ready
- [ ] Hold bride's bouquet during ceremony
- [ ] Offer ongoing support throughout the day!
- [ ]
- [ ]
- [ ]

NOTES

Wedding Day Kit

FOR MAKEUP TOUCH UPS
☐ Concealer
☐ Bronzer
☐ Highlighter
☐ Powder
☐ Eyeshadow
☐ Eyeliner
☐ Lipstick
☐ Lip balm
☐ Compact Mirror
☐ Tweezers
☐ Nail File
☐
☐
☐
☐
☐
☐
☐

FOR HAIR TOUCH UPS
☐ Hairspray
☐ Bobby pins
☐ Hair clips/ties
☐ Brush
☐ Curling Iron
☐ Straightener
☐
☐
☐
☐
☐
☐
☐
☐
☐
☐
☐
☐

FOR WARDROBE
☐ Sewing Kit
☐ Lint Roller
☐ Safety Pins
☐ Small Scissors
☐
☐
☐
☐
☐
☐
☐
☐
☐
☐
☐
☐
☐

NOTES

NOTES

NOTES

Wedding Day Kit

FOR FRESHENING UP
☐ Mouthwash
☐ Toothpaste/Toothbrush
☐ Mints
☐ Chewing gum
☐ Deodorant
☐ Perfume
☐ Tissue/Kleenex
☐
☐
☐
☐
☐
☐
☐
☐
☐
☐
☐

FOR MEDICAL NEEDS
☐ Advil or Tylenol
☐ Pepto-Bismol
☐ Band-Aids
☐ Sunscreen
☐
☐
☐
☐
☐
☐
☐
☐
☐
☐
☐
☐
☐

OTHER
☐ Phone charger
☐ Cash
☐ Hand sanitizer
☐
☐
☐
☐
☐
☐
☐
☐
☐
☐
☐
☐
☐
☐

NOTES

NOTES

NOTES

Wedding Day Kit

☐
☐
☐
☐
☐
☐
☐
☐
☐
☐
☐
☐
☐
☐
☐
☐
☐
☐

☐
☐
☐
☐
☐
☐
☐
☐
☐
☐
☐
☐
☐
☐
☐
☐
☐
☐

☐
☐
☐
☐
☐
☐
☐
☐
☐
☐
☐
☐
☐
☐
☐
☐
☐

NOTES

NOTES

NOTES

Beauty Planner

HAIR

HAIR STYLE	
SALON NAME	
STYLIST NAME	
STYLE IDEAS	
DEPOSIT	
TOTAL COST	

MAKEUP

SALON	
MAKEUP ARTIST	
ADDRESS	
CONSULTATION	
DEPOSIT	
TOTAL COST	

NAILS

SALON	
CONTACT	
STYLE	
CONSULTATION	
DEPOSIT	
TOTAL COST	

SPA/OTHER

DAY OF WEDDING APPOINTMENT TIMES

HAIR :	NAILS:	MAKEUP:

DAY OF WEDDING APPOINTMENT TIMES

Wedding Attire

HELP THE BRIDE SHOP! - POSSIBLE BRIDESMAID DRESS VENDORS

VENDOR	APPOINTMENT	ADDRESS	PHONE

POSSIBLE BRIDAL GOWN VENDORS

VENDOR	APPOINTMENT	ADDRESS	PHONE

Dress Details

BRIDAL SHOP INFORMATION

NAME & PHONE	
ADDRESS	
WEBSITE	

FITTING APPOINTMENTS

FIRST FITTING	
SECOND FITTING	
FINAL FITTING	

MAID OF HONOR ATTIRE

DRESS SIZE		**DRESS COLOR**	
DESIGNER		**SHOE SIZE**	
STYLE NUMBER		**SHOE STYLE**	

MAID OF HONOR HAIR & ACCESSORIES

NAILS		**ACCESSORIES**
HAIR STYLE		**HAIR / NAIL SALON APPOINTMENT DETAILS**
JEWELRY		

OTHER IMPORTANT DETAILS & CHECKLIST

			REMINDERS
☐ DRESS ORDERED	☐ ACCESSORIES ORDERED		
☐ DRESS ARRIVED	☐		
☐ DRESS TAILORED	☐		
☐ DRESS FINISHED	☐		
☐ SHOES ORDERED	☐		
☐ SHOES ARRIVED	☐		

NOTES

Maid of Honor Attire

DRESS:

Shop/Store: _____

Contact Details: _____

Order Date: _____

Fitting Date: _____

Dress Details: _____

Pick Up Date: _____

SHOES & ACCESSORIES:

ITEM	DETAILS / COST	RECEIVED?

Bridesmaid Attire

DRESSES:

Shop/Store: _____

Contact Details: _____

Order Date: _____

Fitting Date: _____

Dress Details: _____

Pick Up Date: _____

WHO'S WEARING IT?	SIZE	COLOR	COST

Bridesmaid Attire

SHOES & ACCESSORIES:

ITEM	DETAILS / COST	RECEIVED?

Bridal Party

BRIDE'S PARENTS	CONTACT INFORMATION
	📞 PHONE
	✉️ EMAIL

GROOM'S PARENTS	CONTACT INFORMATION
	📞 PHONE
	✉️ EMAIL

BEST MAN	CONTACT INFORMATION
	📞 PHONE
	✉️ EMAIL

BRIDESMAID	CONTACT INFORMATION
	📞 PHONE
	✉️ EMAIL

BRIDESMAID	CONTACT INFORMATION
	📞 PHONE
	✉️ EMAIL

BRIDESMAID	CONTACT INFORMATION
	📞 PHONE
	✉️ EMAIL

GROOMSMAN	CONTACT INFORMATION
	📞 PHONE
	✉️ EMAIL

GROOMSMAN	CONTACT INFORMATION
	📞 PHONE
	✉️ EMAIL

GROOMSMAN	CONTACT INFORMATION
	📞 PHONE
	✉️ EMAIL

Bridal Party

		CONTACT INFORMATION
		📞 PHONE
		✉️ EMAIL

		CONTACT INFORMATION
		📞 PHONE
		✉️ EMAIL

		CONTACT INFORMATION
		📞 PHONE
		✉️ EMAIL

		CONTACT INFORMATION
		📞 PHONE
		✉️ EMAIL

		CONTACT INFORMATION
		📞 PHONE
		✉️ EMAIL

		CONTACT INFORMATION
		📞 PHONE
		✉️ EMAIL

		CONTACT INFORMATION
		📞 PHONE
		✉️ EMAIL

		CONTACT INFORMATION
		📞 PHONE
		✉️ EMAIL

		CONTACT INFORMATION
		📞 PHONE
		✉️ EMAIL

Bridal Party

	CONTACT INFORMATION
	📞 PHONE
	✉️ EMAIL

	CONTACT INFORMATION
	📞 PHONE
	✉️ EMAIL

	CONTACT INFORMATION
	📞 PHONE
	✉️ EMAIL

	CONTACT INFORMATION
	📞 PHONE
	✉️ EMAIL

	CONTACT INFORMATION
	📞 PHONE
	✉️ EMAIL

	CONTACT INFORMATION
	📞 PHONE
	✉️ EMAIL

	CONTACT INFORMATION
	📞 PHONE
	✉️ EMAIL

	CONTACT INFORMATION
	📞 PHONE
	✉️ EMAIL

	CONTACT INFORMATION
	📞 PHONE
	✉️ EMAIL

Important Vendors

DRESS VENDOR

👤 NAME

✉ EMAIL

📞 PHONE

HAIR STYLIST / SALON

👤 NAME

✉ EMAIL

📞 PHONE

MAKEUP ARTIST

👤 NAME

✉ EMAIL

📞 PHONE

TAILOR

👤 NAME

✉ EMAIL

📞 PHONE

WEDDING PLANNER

👤 NAME

✉ EMAIL

📞 PHONE

LOCATION OF BRIDAL SHOWER

👤 NAME

✉ EMAIL

📞 PHONE

NAIL SALON

👤 NAME

✉ EMAIL

📞 PHONE

OTHER:

👤 NAME

✉ EMAIL

📞 PHONE

Contact List

👤 NAME	👤 NAME
✉️ EMAIL	✉️ EMAIL
📞 PHONE	📞 PHONE

👤 NAME	👤 NAME
✉️ EMAIL	✉️ EMAIL
📞 PHONE	📞 PHONE

👤 NAME	👤 NAME
✉️ EMAIL	✉️ EMAIL
📞 PHONE	📞 PHONE

👤 NAME	👤 NAME
✉️ EMAIL	✉️ EMAIL
📞 PHONE	📞 PHONE

Contact List

NAME

EMAIL

PHONE

NAME

EMAIL

PHONE

NAME

EMAIL

PHONE

NAME

EMAIL

PHONE

NAME

EMAIL

PHONE

NAME

EMAIL

PHONE

NAME

EMAIL

PHONE

NAME

EMAIL

PHONE

Contact List

👤 **NAME**	👤 **NAME**
✉️ **EMAIL**	✉️ **EMAIL**
📞 **PHONE**	📞 **PHONE**
👤 **NAME**	👤 **NAME**
✉️ **EMAIL**	✉️ **EMAIL**
📞 **PHONE**	📞 **PHONE**
👤 **NAME**	👤 **NAME**
✉️ **EMAIL**	✉️ **EMAIL**
📞 **PHONE**	📞 **PHONE**
👤 **NAME**	👤 **NAME**
✉️ **EMAIL**	✉️ **EMAIL**
📞 **PHONE**	📞 **PHONE**

Wedding Toast Brainstorming

TIPS:

✓ Begin planning and writing your speech around 1 to 2 months prior to the wedding. This will give you time to revise, practice or run it by a friend.

✓ Speech should be around 2-5 minutes long (5 mins maximum)

✓ Write keywords, bullet points, or even the speech on note cards to have on hand as you give the speech.

WHAT TO INCLUDE:

Introduce yourself (your name, your relationship to the bride, how long you've known each other)

Talk about the bride (why she's a good person and friend and share a story to illustrate it)

Tell the love story (the most romantic version of how the bride and groom met if you know it or were involved in their first meeting)

Talk about the groom (Compliment him, why he's great for your friend, what he does for her, etc.)

Celebrate the couple (talk about why they're so good together)

Wish the newlyweds wonderful things for the future

BRAINSTORM IDEAS:

Wedding Toast

Wedding Toast

Wedding Toast

Wedding Toast

Bridal Shower

Idea Board

Write down your thoughts and ideas for the bridal shower!

Bridal Shower Planner

BRIDAL SHOWER DATE

IDEAS, THEME, COLORS

NOTES

VENUE & VENDOR CONTACTS

FOOD & ENTERTAINMENT

NOTES

GUEST LIST

Bridal Shower Planner

GUEST LIST

NOTES

Bridal Shower Budget

NAME	BUDGET	COST	BALANCE DUE	TOTAL SPENT

Bridal Shower Budget

NAME	BUDGET	COST	BALANCE DUE	TOTAL SPENT

Bridal Shower Guests

NAME & CONTACT	RSVP'D		NAME & CONTACT	RSVP'D	
	✗	✔		✗	✔
	✗	✔		✗	✔
	✗	✔		✗	✔
	✗	✔		✗	✔
	✗	✔		✗	✔
	✗	✔		✗	✔
	✗	✔		✗	✔
	✗	✔		✗	✔
	✗	✔		✗	✔
	✗	✔		✗	✔
	✗	✔		✗	✔
	✗	✔		✗	✔
	✗	✔		✗	✔
	✗	✔		✗	✔
	✗	✔		✗	✔
	✗	✔		✗	✔
	✗	✔		✗	✔
	✗	✔		✗	✔
	✗	✔		✗	✔
	✗	✔		✗	✔
	✗	✔		✗	✔
	✗	✔		✗	✔

Bridal Shower Guests

NAME & CONTACT	RSVP'D	
	✕	✔
	✕	✔
	✕	✔
	✕	✔
	✕	✔
	✕	✔
	✕	✔
	✕	✔
	✕	✔
	✕	✔
	✕	✔
	✕	✔
	✕	✔
	✕	✔
	✕	✔
	✕	✔
	✕	✔
	✕	✔
	✕	✔
	✕	✔
	✕	✔
	✕✕	✔

NAME & CONTACT	RSVP'D	
	✕	✔
	✕	✔
	✕	✔
	✕	✔
	✕	✔
	✕	✔
	✕	✔
	✕	✔
	✕	✔
	✕	✔
	✕	✔
	✕	✔
	✕	✔
	✕	✔
	✕	✔
	✕	✔
	✕	✔
	✕	✔
	✕	✔

Bridal Shower Guests

NAME & CONTACT	RSVP'D	
	✕	✔
	✕	✔
	✕	✔
	✕	✔
	✕	✔
	✕	✔
	✕	✔
	✕	✔
	✕	✔
	✕	✔
	✕	✔
	✕	✔
	✕	✔
	✕	✔
	✕	✔
	✕	✔
	✕	✔
	✕	✔
	✕	✔
	✕	✔
	✕	✔
	✕	✔

NAME & CONTACT	RSVP'D	
	✕	✔
	✕	✔
	✕	✔
	✕	✔
	✕	✔
	✕	✔
	✕	✔
	✕	✔
	✕	✔
	✕	✔
	✕	✔
	✕	✔
	✕	✔
	✕	✔
	✕	✔
	✕	✔
	✕	✔
	✕	✔
	✕	✔
	✕	✔
	✕	✔
	✕	✔

Bridal Shower Guests

NAME & CONTACT	RSVP'D		NAME & CONTACT	RSVP'D	
	✗	✔		✗	✔
	✗	✔		✗	✔
	✗	✔		✗	✔
	✗	✔		✗	✔
	✗	✔		✗	✔
	✗	✔		✗	✔
	✗	✔		✗	✔
	✗	✔		✗	✔
	✗	✔		✗	✔
	✗	✔		✗	✔
	✗	✔		✗	✔
	✗	✔		✗	✔
	✗	✔		✗	✔
	✗	✔		✗	✔
	✗	✔		✗	✔
	✗	✔		✗	✔
	✗	✔		✗	✔
	✗	✔		✗	✔
	✗	✔		✗	✔
	✗	✔		✗	✔
	✗	✔		✗	✔
	✗	✔		✗	✔

Timeline & Itinerary

DATE	TIME	DESCRIPTION	NOTES

Timeline & Itinerary

DATE	TIME	DESCRIPTION	NOTES

Shopping List

QTY	FOOD & DRINKS

QTY	PARTY DECOR

QTY	GIFTS

QTY	MISC

Shopping List

QTY	

QTY	

QTY	

QTY	

Shopping List

QTY	

QTY	

QTY	

QTY	

Bachelorette Party

Idea Board

Write down your thoughts and ideas for the bachelorette party!

Bachelorette Party Budget

NAME	BUDGET	COST	BALANCE DUE	TOTAL SPENT

Bachelorette Party Budget

NAME	BUDGET	COST	BALANCE DUE	TOTAL SPENT

Bachelorette Party Budget

NAME	BUDGET	COST	BALANCE DUE	TOTAL SPENT

Bachelorette Party Planning

DATE:	LOCATION:

4-6 MONTHS BEFORE	3-4 MONTHS BEFORE	REMINDERS

2-4 WEEKS BEFORE

WEEK BEFORE

DAY OF BACHELORETTE PARTY

Bachelorette Party Details

DATE:	START TIME:

IMPORTANT CONTACTS

TIME	KEY EVENTS	BOOKED

ACCOMODATION DETAILS

LOCATION NAME:	DIRECTIONS:
ADDRESS:	PHONE CONTACT:
CHECK IN TIME:	CHECK OUT TIME:

NOTES

Bachelorette Guests

NAME & CONTACT	RSVP'D	
	✗	✔
	✗	✔
	✗	✔
	✗	✔
	✗	✔
	✗	✔
	✗	✔
	✗	✔
	✗	✔
	✗	✔
	✗	✔
	✗	✔
	✗	✔
	✗	✔
	✗	✔
	✗	✔
	✗	✔
	✗	✔
	✗	✔
	✗	✔
	✗	✔

NAME & CONTACT	RSVP'D	
	✗	✔
	✗	✔
	✗	✔
	✗	✔
	✗	✔
	✗	✔
	✗	✔
	✗	✔
	✗	✔
	✗	✔
	✗	✔
	✗	✔
	✗	✔
	✗	✔
	✗	✔
	✗	✔
	✗	✔
	✗	✔
	✗	✔
	✗	✔
	✗	✔

Timeline & Itinerary

DATE	TIME	DESCRIPTION	NOTES

Timeline & Itinerary

DATE	TIME	DESCRIPTION	NOTES

Shopping List

QTY	FOOD & DRINKS

QTY	PARTY DECOR

QTY	GIFTS

QTY	MISC

Shopping List

QTY	

QTY	

QTY	

QTY	

Monthly Planner

MONTH OF

MON	TUE	WED	THU	FRI	SAT	SUN

NOTES

Monthly Planner

MONTH OF

MON	TUE	WED	THU	FRI	SAT	SUN

NOTES

Monthly Planner

MONTH OF

MON	TUE	WED	THU	FRI	SAT	SUN

NOTES

Monthly Planner

MONTH OF

MON	TUE	WED	THU	FRI	SAT	SUN

NOTES

Monthly Planner

MONTH OF

MON	TUE	WED	THU	FRI	SAT	SUN

NOTES

Monthly Planner

MONTH OF

MON	TUE	WED	THU	FRI	SAT	SUN

NOTES

Monthly Planner

MONTH OF

MON	TUE	WED	THU	FRI	SAT	SUN

NOTES

Monthly Planner

MONTH OF

MON	TUE	WED	THU	FRI	SAT	SUN

NOTES

Monthly Planner

MONTH OF

MON	TUE	WED	THU	FRI	SAT	SUN

NOTES

Monthly Planner

MONTH OF

MON	TUE	WED	THU	FRI	SAT	SUN

NOTES

Monthly Planner

MONTH OF

MON	TUE	WED	THU	FRI	SAT	SUN

NOTES

Monthly Planner

MONTH OF

MON	TUE	WED	THU	FRI	SAT	SUN

NOTES

Weekly Planner

WEEK OF

MONDAY

TOP PRIORITIES

TUESDAY

TOP PRIORITIES

WEDNESDAY

TOP PRIORITIES

THURSDAY

TOP PRIORITIES

FRIDAY

TOP PRIORITIES

SATURDAY

TOP PRIORITIES

SUNDAY

TOP PRIORITIES

Weekly Planner

WEEK OF

MONDAY

TOP PRIORITIES

TUESDAY

TOP PRIORITIES

WEDNESDAY

TOP PRIORITIES

THURSDAY

TOP PRIORITIES

FRIDAY

TOP PRIORITIES

SATURDAY

TOP PRIORITIES

SUNDAY

TOP PRIORITIES

Weekly Planner

WEEK OF

MONDAY

TOP PRIORITIES

TUESDAY

TOP PRIORITIES

WEDNESDAY

TOP PRIORITIES

THURSDAY

TOP PRIORITIES

FRIDAY

TOP PRIORITIES

SATURDAY

TOP PRIORITIES

SUNDAY

TOP PRIORITIES

Weekly Planner

WEEK OF

MONDAY   **TOP PRIORITIES**

TUESDAY   **TOP PRIORITIES**

WEDNESDAY   **TOP PRIORITIES**

THURSDAY   **TOP PRIORITIES**

FRIDAY   **TOP PRIORITIES**

SATURDAY   **TOP PRIORITIES**

SUNDAY   **TOP PRIORITIES**

Weekly Planner

WEEK OF

MONDAY   **TOP PRIORITIES**

TUESDAY   **TOP PRIORITIES**

WEDNESDAY   **TOP PRIORITIES**

THURSDAY   **TOP PRIORITIES**

FRIDAY   **TOP PRIORITIES**

SATURDAY   **TOP PRIORITIES**

SUNDAY   **TOP PRIORITIES**

Weekly Planner

WEEK OF

MONDAY

TOP PRIORITIES

TUESDAY

TOP PRIORITIES

WEDNESDAY

TOP PRIORITIES

THURSDAY

TOP PRIORITIES

FRIDAY

TOP PRIORITIES

SATURDAY

TOP PRIORITIES

SUNDAY

TOP PRIORITIES

Weekly Planner

WEEK OF

MONDAY

TOP PRIORITIES

TUESDAY

TOP PRIORITIES

WEDNESDAY

TOP PRIORITIES

THURSDAY

TOP PRIORITIES

FRIDAY

TOP PRIORITIES

SATURDAY

TOP PRIORITIES

SUNDAY

TOP PRIORITIES

WEEK OF

MONDAY	TOP PRIORITIES

TUESDAY	TOP PRIORITIES

WEDNESDAY	TOP PRIORITIES

THURSDAY	TOP PRIORITIES

FRIDAY	TOP PRIORITIES

SATURDAY	TOP PRIORITIES

SUNDAY	TOP PRIORITIES

Weekly Planner

MONDAY

TOP PRIORITIES

TUESDAY

TOP PRIORITIES

WEDNESDAY

TOP PRIORITIES

THURSDAY

TOP PRIORITIES

FRIDAY

TOP PRIORITIES

SATURDAY

TOP PRIORITIES

SUNDAY

TOP PRIORITIES

Weekly Planner

WEEK OF

MONDAY   **TOP PRIORITIES**

TUESDAY   **TOP PRIORITIES**

WEDNESDAY   **TOP PRIORITIES**

THURSDAY   **TOP PRIORITIES**

FRIDAY   **TOP PRIORITIES**

SATURDAY   **TOP PRIORITIES**

SUNDAY   **TOP PRIORITIES**

Weekly Planner

WEEK OF

MONDAY   TOP PRIORITIES

TUESDAY   TOP PRIORITIES

WEDNESDAY   TOP PRIORITIES

THURSDAY   TOP PRIORITIES

FRIDAY   TOP PRIORITIES

SATURDAY   TOP PRIORITIES

SUNDAY   TOP PRIORITIES

WEEK OF

MONDAY   TOP PRIORITIES

TUESDAY   TOP PRIORITIES

WEDNESDAY   TOP PRIORITIES

THURSDAY   TOP PRIORITIES

FRIDAY   TOP PRIORITIES

SATURDAY   TOP PRIORITIES

SUNDAY   TOP PRIORITIES

WEEK OF

MONDAY　　　　　　　　　　　　　TOP PRIORITIES

TUESDAY　　　　　　　　　　　　　TOP PRIORITIES

WEDNESDAY　　　　　　　　　　　　TOP PRIORITIES

THURSDAY　　　　　　　　　　　　TOP PRIORITIES

FRIDAY　　　　　　　　　　　　　TOP PRIORITIES

SATURDAY　　　　　　　　　　　　TOP PRIORITIES

SUNDAY　　　　　　　　　　　　　TOP PRIORITIES

WEEK OF

MONDAY   TOP PRIORITIES

TUESDAY   TOP PRIORITIES

WEDNESDAY   TOP PRIORITIES

THURSDAY   TOP PRIORITIES

FRIDAY   TOP PRIORITIES

SATURDAY   TOP PRIORITIES

SUNDAY   TOP PRIORITIES

Weekly Planner

WEEK OF

MONDAY

TOP PRIORITIES

TUESDAY

TOP PRIORITIES

WEDNESDAY

TOP PRIORITIES

THURSDAY

TOP PRIORITIES

FRIDAY

TOP PRIORITIES

SATURDAY

TOP PRIORITIES

SUNDAY

TOP PRIORITIES

Weekly Planner

WEEK OF

MONDAY   TOP PRIORITIES

TUESDAY   TOP PRIORITIES

WEDNESDAY   TOP PRIORITIES

THURSDAY   TOP PRIORITIES

FRIDAY   TOP PRIORITIES

SATURDAY   TOP PRIORITIES

SUNDAY   TOP PRIORITIES

WEEK OF

MONDAY

TOP PRIORITIES

TUESDAY

TOP PRIORITIES

WEDNESDAY

TOP PRIORITIES

THURSDAY

TOP PRIORITIES

FRIDAY

TOP PRIORITIES

SATURDAY

TOP PRIORITIES

SUNDAY

TOP PRIORITIES

WEEK OF

MONDAY   TOP PRIORITIES

TUESDAY   TOP PRIORITIES

WEDNESDAY   TOP PRIORITIES

THURSDAY   TOP PRIORITIES

FRIDAY   TOP PRIORITIES

SATURDAY   TOP PRIORITIES

SUNDAY   TOP PRIORITIES

Weekly Planner

WEEK OF

MONDAY

TOP PRIORITIES

TUESDAY

TOP PRIORITIES

WEDNESDAY

TOP PRIORITIES

THURSDAY

TOP PRIORITIES

FRIDAY

TOP PRIORITIES

SATURDAY

TOP PRIORITIES

SUNDAY

TOP PRIORITIES

Weekly Planner

WEEK OF

MONDAY

TOP PRIORITIES

TUESDAY

TOP PRIORITIES

WEDNESDAY

TOP PRIORITIES

THURSDAY

TOP PRIORITIES

FRIDAY

TOP PRIORITIES

SATURDAY

TOP PRIORITIES

SUNDAY

TOP PRIORITIES

Weekly Planner

WEEK OF

MONDAY

TOP PRIORITIES

TUESDAY

TOP PRIORITIES

WEDNESDAY

TOP PRIORITIES

THURSDAY

TOP PRIORITIES

FRIDAY

TOP PRIORITIES

SATURDAY

TOP PRIORITIES

SUNDAY

TOP PRIORITIES

Weekly Planner

WEEK OF

MONDAY	TOP PRIORITIES

TUESDAY	TOP PRIORITIES

WEDNESDAY	TOP PRIORITIES

THURSDAY	TOP PRIORITIES

FRIDAY	TOP PRIORITIES

SATURDAY	TOP PRIORITIES

SUNDAY	TOP PRIORITIES

 **Weekly Planner**

WEEK OF

MONDAY

TOP PRIORITIES

TUESDAY

TOP PRIORITIES

WEDNESDAY

TOP PRIORITIES

THURSDAY

TOP PRIORITIES

FRIDAY

TOP PRIORITIES

SATURDAY

TOP PRIORITIES

SUNDAY

TOP PRIORITIES

Weekly Planner

WEEK OF

MONDAY   TOP PRIORITIES

TUESDAY   TOP PRIORITIES

WEDNESDAY   TOP PRIORITIES

THURSDAY   TOP PRIORITIES

FRIDAY   TOP PRIORITIES

SATURDAY   TOP PRIORITIES

SUNDAY   TOP PRIORITIES

Weekly Planner

WEEK OF

MONDAY

TOP PRIORITIES

TUESDAY

TOP PRIORITIES

WEDNESDAY

TOP PRIORITIES

THURSDAY

TOP PRIORITIES

FRIDAY

TOP PRIORITIES

SATURDAY

TOP PRIORITIES

SUNDAY

TOP PRIORITIES

WEEK OF [   ]

MONDAY   TOP PRIORITIES

TUESDAY   TOP PRIORITIES

WEDNESDAY   TOP PRIORITIES

THURSDAY   TOP PRIORITIES

FRIDAY   TOP PRIORITIES

SATURDAY   TOP PRIORITIES

SUNDAY   TOP PRIORITIES

Weekly Planner

MONDAY

TOP PRIORITIES

TUESDAY

TOP PRIORITIES

WEDNESDAY

TOP PRIORITIES

THURSDAY

TOP PRIORITIES

FRIDAY

TOP PRIORITIES

SATURDAY

TOP PRIORITIES

SUNDAY

TOP PRIORITIES

WEEK OF

MONDAY   TOP PRIORITIES

TUESDAY   TOP PRIORITIES

WEDNESDAY   TOP PRIORITIES

THURSDAY   TOP PRIORITIES

FRIDAY   TOP PRIORITIES

SATURDAY   TOP PRIORITIES

SUNDAY   TOP PRIORITIES

Weekly Planner

WEEK OF

MONDAY

TOP PRIORITIES

TUESDAY

TOP PRIORITIES

WEDNESDAY

TOP PRIORITIES

THURSDAY

TOP PRIORITIES

FRIDAY

TOP PRIORITIES

SATURDAY

TOP PRIORITIES

SUNDAY

TOP PRIORITIES

Weekly Planner

WEEK OF

MONDAY
TOP PRIORITIES

TUESDAY
TOP PRIORITIES

WEDNESDAY
TOP PRIORITIES

THURSDAY
TOP PRIORITIES

FRIDAY
TOP PRIORITIES

SATURDAY
TOP PRIORITIES

SUNDAY
TOP PRIORITIES

Weekly Planner

MONDAY

TOP PRIORITIES

TUESDAY

TOP PRIORITIES

WEDNESDAY

TOP PRIORITIES

THURSDAY

TOP PRIORITIES

FRIDAY

TOP PRIORITIES

SATURDAY

TOP PRIORITIES

SUNDAY

TOP PRIORITIES

WEEK OF

MONDAY   **TOP PRIORITIES**

TUESDAY   **TOP PRIORITIES**

WEDNESDAY   **TOP PRIORITIES**

THURSDAY   **TOP PRIORITIES**

FRIDAY   **TOP PRIORITIES**

SATURDAY   **TOP PRIORITIES**

SUNDAY   **TOP PRIORITIES**

WEEK OF

MONDAY

TOP PRIORITIES

TUESDAY

TOP PRIORITIES

WEDNESDAY

TOP PRIORITIES

THURSDAY

TOP PRIORITIES

FRIDAY

TOP PRIORITIES

SATURDAY

TOP PRIORITIES

SUNDAY

TOP PRIORITIES

Weekly Planner

WEEK OF

MONDAY | TOP PRIORITIES

TUESDAY | TOP PRIORITIES

WEDNESDAY | TOP PRIORITIES

THURSDAY | TOP PRIORITIES

FRIDAY | TOP PRIORITIES

SATURDAY | TOP PRIORITIES

SUNDAY | TOP PRIORITIES

Notes / To Do's / Etc.

Notes / To Do's / Etc.

Notes / To Do's / Etc.

Notes / To Do's / Etc.

Notes / To Do's / Etc.

Notes / To Do's / Etc.

Notes / To Do's / Etc.

Notes / To Do's / Etc.

Notes / To Do's / Etc.

Notes / To Do's / Etc.

Notes / To Do's / Etc.

Notes / To Do's / Etc.

Notes / To Do's / Etc.

Notes / To Do's / Etc.

Notes / To Do's / Etc.

Notes / To Do's / Etc.

Notes / To Do's / Etc.

Notes / To Do's / Etc.

Notes / To Do's / Etc.

Notes / To Do's / Etc.

Notes / To Do's / Etc.

Notes / To Do's / Etc.

Notes / To Do's / Etc.

Notes / To Do's / Etc.

Notes / To Do's / Etc.

Notes / To Do's / Etc.

Notes / To Do's / Etc.

Notes / To Do's / Etc.

Made in the USA
Middletown, DE
08 September 2022